PROFILES OF FLIGHT

BRITISH AEROSPACE HAWK

Hawk T.1A XX205 armed with 30 mm ADEN cannon pod on the centre-line and a pair of AIM-9L Sidewinder AAMs under the wings. The Hawk T.1A modification programme for eighty-nine aircraft was completed in May 1986. (BAe)

PROFILES OF FLIGHT

BRITISH AEROSPACE HAWK

ARMED LIGHT ATTACK AND MULTI-COMBAT FIGHTER TRAINER

DAVE WINDLE & MARTIN BOWMAN

Pen & Sword
AVIATION

First published in Great Britain in 2010 by
PEN & SWORD AVIATION
An imprint of
Pen & Sword Books Ltd
47 Church Street
Barnsley
South Yorkshire
S70 2AS

ISBN 978 1 84884 236 6

A CIP catalogue record for this book is
available from the British Library

Printed in China through Printworks Int. Ltd

Pen & Sword Books Ltd incorporates the Imprints of
Pen & Sword Aviation, Pen & Sword Family History, Pen & Sword Maritime,
Pen & Sword Military, Wharncliffe Local History, Pen & Sword Select,
Pen & Sword Military Classics, Leo Cooper, Remember When,
Seaforth Publishing and Frontline Publishing

For a complete list of Pen & Sword titles please contact
PEN & SWORD BOOKS LIMITED
47 Church Street, Barnsley, South Yorkshire, S70 2AS, England
E-mail: enquiries@pen-and-sword.co.uk
Website: www.pen-and-sword.co.uk

ACKNOWLEDGEMENTS

I am indebted to Bernard Noble and his son Kevin Noble for their kind permission to adapt material from *Noble Endeavours (Three Generations of RAF Pilots)* (1998), which details the varied and successful careers of both these remarkable RAF pilots. The vivid descriptions of Hawk training have been adapted from this family 'bible'. Bernard joined the RAF as an apprentice in 1946, and was a serving RAF officer until retirement in 1994 with the rank of squadron leader. Kevin Noble became a Jaguar pilot in RAF Germany, and this period of his remarkable career is featured in *SEPECAT Jaguar: Tactical Support & Maritime Strike Fighter* by Martin W. Bowman (Pen & Sword 2007). His later career on the Panavia Tornado is also featured in the *Profiles of Flight* series. At the time of writing Kevin is a 747 commercial airline captain with British Airways.

Hawk T.1A XX309 at the October Air Show at Duxford in 2005. (Author)

British Aerospace Hawk

'While the Hawk may not have either the classical elegance of the Hunter or the nimble agility of the Gnat,' wrote one senior RAF training officer and former Red Arrows pilot, 'the Hawk is a very versatile aircraft and effective advanced trainer.' Air Staff Target (AST) 362 was issued in 1964 for a new high-performance trainer to replace the Hawker Siddeley Gnat and the Hunter T.7, as well as certain Jet Provost roles, in service with the Royal Air Force. At that time the requirement was only partially filled by a small number of two-seat SEPECAT Jaguar aircraft. The decision was taken to abandon the idea of a high-performance trainer, and the requirement changed to that of a subsonic aircraft. In 1968 Hawker Siddeley Aviation Ltd at Kingston-on-Thames and Dunsfold, Surrey, a company with a vast experience of building military training aircraft, initiated studies for such a trainer, and the company's private venture P.1182 (later HS.1182) evolved into an advanced trainer formalised as AST 397 in January 1970. In October 1971 Hawker Siddeley emerged successful from a Ministry of Defence competition with a project known as the HS.1182,

A Hawk T.1 of 4 FTS RAF Valley, passing the Menai Bridge. (MoD)

Six Hawks flying in formation as Farnborough '76 opened. The second aircraft in formation is the civil-registered company demonstrator, G-HAWK (ZA101), making its public debut at Farnborough. (Hawker Siddeley)

and in April 1972 it was awarded a production contract for a total of 175 Hawk T.1s. There were no prototypes or pre-production aircraft, five of the six aircraft used for flight development being scheduled to be refurbished for delivery to the RAF as part of the production order. The last of these was delivered to the RAF on 17 March 1982, the last production aircraft (XX353) having been handed over on 9 February that same year.

The design team opted for a simple but robust low-wing layout for an aircraft of modest dimensions, though much larger than the Gnat, and powered by a Rolls-Royce/Turboméca Adour Mk 151-01 low-bypass turbofan engine rated at 5,200 lb. In reheated form, two of these engines powered the Jaguar strike/attack aircraft, but the 151-01 is unaugmented. Hawk construction is entirely conventional: the fuselage incorporates skin, stringer and frame components; the one-piece wing is attached by three bolts on each side, which places the associated structure under compression for integral strength; inboard of the 'kink' in the leading edge, the wing encloses an integral fuel tank and pick-up points for the main landing-gear units; and three hard-points (one under the fuselage and two under the wing) were fitted as standard on RAF machines. The wing's hydraulically powered ailerons and three-position, double-slotted flaps are complemented by an air brake below the rear fuselage. Historically, the Hawk was the first British aircraft to be designed from the outset using the metric system of measurement. It was also the first British tandem-seat trainer to offer the ideal forward visibility for the instructor in the high-mounted rear seat, well above the pupil in the front seat, to provide him with excellent forward fields of vision.

The first Hawk T.Mk 1 (XX154) was rolled out at Dunsfold on 12 August 1974, and it flew for the first time on 21 August. Subsequently, it appeared at the Farnborough Air Show the following month. The second aircraft (XX157) flew on 22 April 1975. Flight testing demonstrated that the Hawk exceeded all its performance requirements: although supersonic performance was not specified, XX154 reached Mach 1.04 in a shallow dive on 26 February 1975. The new aircraft would be 'red lined' at Mach=1.2 thanks to careful wing design. (Despite having two engines to the Hawk's one, the Franco-German Alpha Jet is limited to speeds below about Mach=0.9.) The first Hawk T.Mk 1 (XX161) was delivered to RAF Valley on the Isle of

Anglesey on 1 April 1976, where the Hawk would supersede the Gnat at No. 4 Flying Training School (FTS), but it was not until 4 November 1976 that same year that the next two aircraft were officially handed over. At No. 4 FTS students began a total of seventy-five hours' dual and solo instruction on the new aircraft. At least ten hours in the advanced training syllabus was eliminated by removing the need for the Hunter in its advanced weapon training role, as the Hawk was able to undertake the weapons phase previously handled by the Hawker Hunter. Valley's initial course of pilots graduated in November 1977.

Wing Commander Ian C. H. Dick MBE AFC of the Air Staff at HQ RAF Training Command, and a former leader of the Red Arrows display team, evaluated the Hawk in the late 1970s. He found that the Hawk had

> an undeniably good lifting wing and a superb view from the rear cockpit. Here was an aircraft designed from the outset as a trainer not only with features to make training straightforward and effective but also with the ability to be developed in a number of operational roles. The seat is very comfortable and two-hour sorties can be completed without any discomfort or fatigue being felt in any way. The Hawk flies comfortably at low level throughout the useful speed range of 220 to 500 knots. Look-out is excellent from both cockpits and instrumentation is adequate for accurate pegging of speed and heading. Owing to the sensitive efficiency of the wing and its low loading, turbulence can unsettle the aircraft and lead to a rough ride even at medium levels, where such disturbance is felt as a mild vibration. This feature makes steady formation flying a challenge. However, the aircraft responds quickly and positively to small control movements, and so accurate position keeping is not likely to prove too great a problem. More significant for the Red Arrows is the slightly slower throttle response because of the twin-spool engine. [Later, the Red Arrows Hawks had their engines modified to 151-02 standard for faster throttle-response power, output remaining unaltered.] The present remarkably crisp formation changes of the team rely, to a great extent, on the unusually snappy response of the Gnat's engine. Future Red Arrows pilots will, therefore, need to anticipate to a greater extent their power changes. Nevertheless, the Hawk is generally pleasing to fly in formation throughout the speed range. Selection of the services presents no problems, and formation circuits, approaches and landings are straightforward. Tail chasing can prove a challenge – particularly when it tightens up – as one is

seeking the best turning performance to hold a good position while avoiding too much buffet. The aircraft appears to ride slipstream surprisingly well.

There is nothing unusual or difficult about flying the Hawk in the circuit. The instructor, overwhelmed by his unprecedented view from the rear cockpit, takes a little time to adjust to the apparent nose-down attitude on the approach. Otherwise, circuit flying follows a standard pattern with a downwind speed of 190 knots, decreasing to 150 knots by the end of the downwind leg and 130 knots

Hawk T.1 XX157, the second Hawk production aircraft, which flew on 22 April 1975, with MATRA 155 launch pods containing up to eighteen spin-stabilised rockets of 68 mm calibre under the wings. In weapons training one pod was usually fitted beneath the Hawk's starboard wing. On the Hawk's port wing inner pylon would be an ML Aviation CBLS 100 Mk 1 launcher for practice-bombs. (BAe)

straight in at the end of the final turn; the threshold speed is 110 knots plus one knot for every 220 lb of fuel. With the relatively slow acceleration of the engine, it is important that rpm are kept up around 70% during the approach to land, but this requirement is helped by the powerful drag force produced from extending full flap. On rolling or overshooting, the lifting power of the wing with full slotted flaps is an experience to behold; the additional flap lift is supreme, and an impressive 1,000 feet of height can be gained by the end of a 2,000-yard runway. This is clearly where the flaps come into their own – as a low speed aid; they are not designed for use in manoeuvring over 200 knots. Instrument flying is a simple process in the Hawk. Having landed the aircraft, stopping it – unassisted by any brake parachute – requires the same knack of braking technique used for taxiing. Climbing out of the Hawk after one's first sortie, there is the compelling urge to get back in and do it all again.

By the summer of 1978, Hawker had completed production of a hundred out of its total order of 175 Hawks for the RAF, which by that time had fifty in

The civil-registered company demonstrator, G-HAWK (ZA101), in desert scheme flying low during flight-development trials in the Middle East. (Hawker Siddeley)

Hawk T.1 XX156 over the Pyramids at Giza near Cairo in Egypt. There were no prototypes or pre-production aircraft, five of the six aircraft used for flight development being scheduled to be refurbished for delivery to the RAF as part of the production order. (BAe)

service. The Hawk also entered service as a Hunter replacement at the No. 1 Tactical Weapons Unit at RAF Brawdy. Other users were No. 2 TWU at RAF Lossiemouth, and later RAF Chivenor, the Central Flying School at Valley (and later at RAF Scampton), the Empire Test Pilots School at Boscombe Down, and of course the Red Arrows aerobatic team. During the first ten years as the RAF's aerobatic team, it gave 850 displays, and the 1,000th performance came in 1977. By the end of the 1979 season, when the Gnats were scheduled to be replaced by the new BAe Hawk T.1, the team had given 1,292 public performances, involving visits to eighteen overseas countries. The Red Arrows took delivery of the Hawk in the winter of 1979/80, setting Squadron Leader Brian Hoskins the task of seeing through the conversion of the pilots from Gnat to Hawk, introducing two new team members and working up a display using a new aeroplane in time for the start of the 1980 season. The fact that the team was ready to display on time was not only a tribute to the pilots and ground crew, but also evidence that the Hawk would

BAe Hawk 51A HW-338 in Finnish Air Force markings. (BAe)

be a worthy successor to the Gnat. Through this decade the Red Arrows flew the Hawk, not only in Britain and Europe, but also on major tours to North America, the Middle East and Scandinavia. The most ambitious tour, to the Far East, was completed in 1986. It involved giving twenty-two displays in fifteen countries, and travelling 18,500 miles in six weeks. By the end of the 1988 season, the Red Arrows had completed 2,313 public displays. In time of war the red aircraft would be camouflaged, armed with 30 mm cannon and Sidewinder missiles, and flown by the ten team pilots to augment the UK air defence forces.

Today's fast-jet pilots in the RAF who fly aircraft like the Tornado and Eurofighter Typhoon will have all graduated from a long training process, completing Elementary Flying Training, then Basic, where they fly the Tucano T1, and finally the Hawk T.1/1A in Advanced at RAF Valley. In 1982 the process was very different. A young acting pilot officer, after successfully completing an eighteen-week Initial Officer Training Course at RAF Cranwell in Lincolnshire, and undergoing Aviation Medicine training at RAF North Luffenham, would take his place at a basic flying training school (BFTS) for pilot training on the Jet Provost Mk 3. Successful students then graduated to No. 4 FTS at Valley, where the first four weeks would be spent in the ground school, learning about the Hawk and its systems and doing exercises in the flight simulator, which included learning a new set of checks by heart. By this time pilots would have all learned the value of doing as much ground preparation as possible in order to make life easier when they started flying.

Kevin Noble, who was one of the pilots on the course at 4 FTS in the winter of 1982, will now take us through the training syllabus.

> The watch-word apparently was 'P6' – 'Prior Preparation Prevents Piss-Poor Performance'. The Hawk checklist was much thicker than that of the Jet Provost, as with a more complicated aircraft there were more drills and emergencies to learn. Towards the end of the ground school, both courses went on a survival expedition in Snowdonia. The scenario was that they had ejected into enemy territory and had to survive for four days on what they would have in these circumstances. This comprised a parachute, dinghy, flying kit and survival rations, which consisted of one small tin of sweets. To provide protection from the elements, each of us constructed a bivouac and a sleeping bag, using only brushwood and pieces of parachute.

Surprisingly, we were not bothered by hunger, but everything became an effort because of the lack of energy. Each day we were given a task to navigate across country following a specified route, and this culminated in an escape and evasion exercise on the last night. For the latter we had to reach a rendezvous held by friendly forces while avoiding the enemy who were looking for us. It rained for most of the four days, so we were all very cold, wet and weary by the last night, which was totally overcast with steady rain. Additionally, there were no lights in that remote mountain area, and at best one could not see more than a few feet. In the woods it was impossible to see a hand in front of the face. One of the course fell over a thirty-foot cliff and fractured his spine and skull. He was off flying for several months and became permanently deaf in one ear, since a nerve had been severed. Nevertheless, he eventually returned to fly Puma helicopters, and later transferred to fast jets on the Tornado F3. We were all very glad to get into a warm bus at the end of the exercise and to go back to Valley for a hot bath and bed. Not surprisingly, after the bath I discovered that my pile of clothing stank of wood smoke from the fires we lit for warmth and from my not having washed or changed for four days.

My first flight on the course was a thirty-five-minute familiarisation trip in a Hawk on 22 March 1982. The Hawk was a major change from side-by-side to tandem seating; sitting alone in the front cockpit it felt much more like a fighter, and first impressions were that it was much faster, with impressive acceleration and climb rate. The ailerons and tailplane were power operated and were very responsive at medium and high speeds, making the aircraft a delight to fly; the rudder, which was little used, was manually operated. At first, wearing the 'g' suit felt rather strange, but I rapidly became used to it. This first trip passed very quickly as the instructor demonstrated general handling (GH) followed by flight at low level. The latter was at 420 knots and was noticeably much quicker than in the Jet Provost. I also noticed that to turn at this speed, applying bank and light back pressure on the stick was ineffective; it was necessary to apply at least 60° of bank and pull. The low-level flight culminated with a run up the A5 towards Anglesey at 250 feet. Initially it appeared that the valley ended at a mountain face and that we would have to pull up, but at the last moment it dropped away through a sharp 90° turn to the right. At this point the instructor rolled to 135° of bank, so that the aircraft was half-way to being on its back, and pulled down to fly a tight turn to the right while

A BAe Hawk 200 armed with four AIM-9L Sidewinder AAMs and an inbuilt pair of 25 mm ADEN cannon under the cockpit floor. (BAe)

descending over a lip into the valley, rolling upright as we entered the final stretch leading up to the Menai Straits. It was exhilarating to see the rocks flashing past just a couple of hundred feet away, and during the last part of the manoeuvre we were below the road and looking up at the traffic. Approaching Menai the instructor pulled up to 3,000 feet for the return to Valley. This was a very exciting introduction to flying on the course, and it whetted my appetite for more.

The next few sorties covered elementary handling, stalling, aerobatics, circuits and instrument flying (IF) and, weather permitting, most were flown over North Wales and the Lleyn Peninsula. Aerobatics in the Hawk were very different from those in the Jet Provost. The greater speed needed much more room; for example a loop required 4–5 'g' at the pull-up, and 5,000 feet of vertical airspace, and a considerable amount of 'g' was needed for any turning manoeuvres at high speed. Fortunately the Adour engine gave plenty of power and was very efficient, so that with its good fuel capacity the Hawk had a typical sortie length of 60–70 minutes. The wing produced plenty of lift without a large increase in induced drag, and the Hawk was renowned for being able to sustain up to 6–7 'g' at low level without loss of speed. About the only normal aerobatic manoeuvre for which it was not cleared was the stall turn. After nine hours' dual instruction, I made my first solo flight on 13 April. Unlike the Jet Provost, where pilots did just one visual circuit and landed after less than five minutes, in the Hawk the pilot did a trip round the island, normally flat out at 550 knots, followed by a few circuits before landing after thirty minutes. The next exercise was spinning, and this again was very different from the Jet Provost. Because of the much greater rate of descent, we had to start at 25,000–30,000 feet, and the Hawk was initially reluctant to enter the spin, which was rather oscillatory, with some shuddering and the nose pitching up and down. Although it was not difficult to enter or recover, care had to be taken not to apply aileron against the direction of spin, as, like any swept-wing aircraft, the rate of rotation then increased and recovery was more difficult. It was probably for this reason that solo spinning by students was prohibited.

Next came practice forced landings (PFL). For its class the Hawk was an excellent glider and could

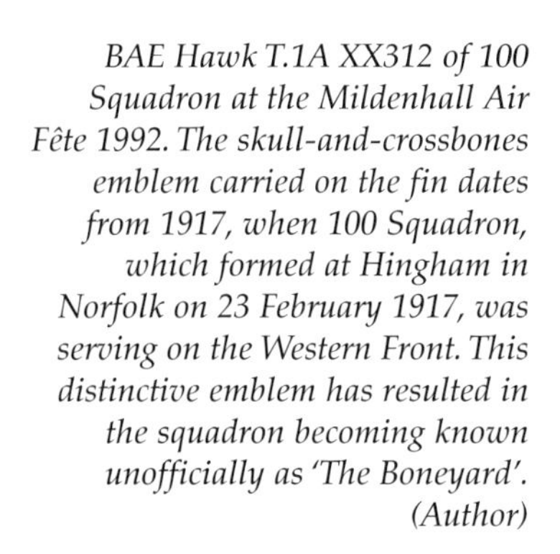

BAE Hawk T.1A XX312 of 100 Squadron at the Mildenhall Air Fête 1992. The skull-and-crossbones emblem carried on the fin dates from 1917, when 100 Squadron, which formed at Hingham in Norfolk on 23 February 1917, was serving on the Western Front. This distinctive emblem has resulted in the squadron becoming known unofficially as 'The Boneyard'. (Author)

cover two miles per 1,000 feet of height lost. The lowering of full flap produced a large increase in drag, and this greatly eased the problem of judging the correct touch-down point on landing. With undercarriage down, the aim was to arrive high on the final approach and lower full flap at the *moment critique*. Then, if necessary, the nose could be pushed down into quite a steep descent without a large increase in airspeed, and with practice I was soon able to achieve reasonable results. After more GH and aerobatics, I moved on to maximum-rate turns; these were similar to those in the Jet Provost, but with higher 'g'. The method was to pull rapidly to 5 'g' and then slowly up to 6 'g', but students often snatched to 6 'g' before going on to 7 'g' or more unless prevented by an alert instructor. Constant repetition of high 'g' soon made us all develop 'Hawk neck'. The neck muscles enlarged to meet the additional load of the combined weights of head and helmet at 6 'g', and this became noticeable when shirt collars started getting tight. During the latter part of April there were more GH sorties, both dual and solo, with up to three flights on a good day. I soon found that this could be quite tiring, especially when sustained high 'g' levels were involved.

I passed my progress check satisfactorily at the end of April and did a couple of IF sorties before the instrument rating test (IRT) in early May. I was then awarded a White Instrument Rating; this was a great improvement on the Amber Rating, as I was now permitted to continue an approach in cloud down to 200 feet above the decision height for the runway and instrument approach aid in use. Unfortunately, one member of the course had difficulties that culminated in his being 'chopped' (failed) on his IRT. He went on to become an Andover pilot.

Low-level navigation at a speed of 420 knots and a height of 250 feet came next. The Hawk was excellent for this task, as, with just 1,350 kg of fuel, most trips lasted around fifty minutes, returning to Valley with minimum landing fuel of 250 kg, which allowed sufficient to divert to the relief landing ground at Mona, some five miles away. On my third low-level navigation trip I experienced the first of several bird strikes during my career. A bird strike presented a serious hazard to high-speed single-engined jet aircraft, especially if it was on the windscreen or down the engine intake. Initial action was to pull up to get away from the ground and lose speed; the throttle was left where it was, as jet engines often continued to function with quite major damage until the throttle was moved. The pilot had then to assess the damage and get visual inspection from another aircraft if possible, before diverting to the nearest airfield. A low-speed handling check was then made at a safe height to assess handling in the approach configuration with undercarriage and flap lowered. This gave the pilot plenty of height to sort out any problems and decide if, and by how much, he needed to increase the speed for his landing approach. If the bird went down the intake into the engine it could often be smelt – rather like roast chicken – as cockpit pressurisation came off the engine compressor. In this case, the pilot would set up a precautionary PFL pattern; then, if the engine failed at a critical stage, he could complete a glide approach and landing.

After three dual low-level navigation trips, I went on my first solo exercise for a fifty-minute sortie. Then came high-low (Hi-Lo) navigation exercises. The first part was flown at high level using radio navigation aids such as Tacan – which gave range and bearing from a selected beacon – to let down to the low-level entry point. This was often Start Point on the south coast of Devon, or St Abb's Head to the north of Newcastle, after which we flew at low level back to base. These trips were of longer duration, usually between seventy-five and eighty minutes, as the jet engine was much more efficient at high level. The Hawk was very good at high level; it could climb rapidly to 40,000 feet or above and cruise up there at better than 1 kg of fuel per mile (nearly four miles per gallon), which was excellent for that sort of aircraft. From 40,000 feet it could then glide for eighty miles or more with the engine at idle. Returning to Valley from Scotland, one could pull up from low level with just 500 kg of fuel remaining to recover to Valley and shut the throttle abeam the Isle of Man. This outstanding range added greatly to the aircraft's flexibility, allowing navigation routes to be flown over most of the UK, wherever the weather happened to be most suitable. On one trip on a clear day at 40,000 feet over Isle of Man, I clearly remember the magnificent view, and could see both the east and west coasts of the UK.

As the Hawk did not have such advanced equipment as an inertial navigation system (INAS) or a moving map which were fitted to operational aircraft, basic low-level navigational techniques relying on maps and stopwatch were used. Navigation routes were planned using a 1:500,000 scale (normally known as a half million) map; this was far too large a scale to find a small target, so the standard 1:50,000 Ordnance Survey map (just over one inch to the mile) was used for the target area. First a suitable attack direction to the target was chosen, ideally with a lead-in feature such as a major road or the edge of a prominent wood, to

BAe Hawk T.1A XX351 in overall high-conspicuity gloss black finish at the Duxford August Air Show in 2005. (Author)

enable the target to be located, even if it was small and well concealed. A large, easily identifiable feature, normally about one minute's flying time (seven or eight miles) from the target, was then selected back along the attack track: this was the initial position (IP). The pilot navigated, using the 'half million' map, to the IP, where he transferred to the 1:50,000 map for the run-up to the target. Accurate navigation could be quite difficult as the aircraft was covering the ground at around a mile every eight seconds, often over strange terrain which had few landmarks or other features. The students found that it was then all too easy to make external features fit those on the map and delude themselves that they were on the right track, only to find they had missed the target. Having overflown the target, navigation was then resumed using the 'half million' map. Efficient map management in the confined space of the cockpit was crucial; all maps had to be properly folded to show the area on either side of the track, and stowed in the correct order in the flying-suit pocket. Dropping a map on the floor could be disastrous. With practice, and using basic map and stopwatch techniques, I was soon able to navigate to small targets and arrive within ten seconds of the required time.

The instructors introduced further complications in flight to increase the workload as the exercises progressed. This usually entailed either rerouteing to a different target, requiring planning of a fresh track, or a simulated emergency, necessitating a practice diversion to the nearest suitable airfield. After several dual and solo navigational trips, I did a low-level navigation exercise with my instructor and three other students with their instructors, to land at Lossiemouth for the night. I thoroughly enjoyed flying in Scotland, with its magnificent scenery, and it is still my favourite place to fly. With all the high ground it was necessary to keep a close watch on the weather, as we frequently flew up valleys towards high ground, with low cloud on the hills. This could be very dangerous, and we always had to be ready to make an early decision to 'abort' by executing a steep climb out on instruments to a safe altitude – up to 6,500 feet over most of Scotland – above the mountains. Happily, on this occasion the weather was good and we had excellent trips both ways, with a very pleasant evening at Lossiemouth.

After a few more navigational exercises, I took my final navigation test in mid-May. The weather *en route* to the Lake District was not good, and I had to pull up from low level and fly a heading and calculated time above cloud before letting down again once the weather had cleared. Fortunately, this worked out nicely and I regained track further north in the Lakes. Cloud on the hills further north-east over the Pennines meant that I had to leave the planned low-level route and navigate my way around the bad weather to regain track. Not having encountered weather like this before, I found this hard work, and soon became 'temporarily uncertain of my position' – a polite way of saying that I was lost. The instructor took control and flew me back onto track so that I could continue from there. This was not what I would have hoped for, and although I passed the test, it was a disappointing end to the navigation phase, which had gone reasonably well to that point. Fortunately, there was no time to brood, as I was off again the same day on the introduction to formation flying. The same principles applied as on the Jet Provost, but closing

Hawk T.1A XX351/CQ, armed with a pair of AIM-9L Sidewinders, in formation with another 100 Squadron T.1A. (MoD)

Hawk T.1A XX313/CE in formation with a Eurofighter Typhoon. (MoD)

speeds were higher in formation join-ups, and the classic student error of approaching the leader with far too much overtaking speed, and overshooting, was repeated. I always enjoyed close-formation flying, and was very happy with this phase.

After three dual formation trips, I did solo formation, and this was followed by a dual trip leading a formation. A session of high-level formation demonstrated that less power and performance were available and that more anticipation and smoothness were required to achieve acceptable results. After a couple more solo close-formation trips, we moved on to tactical (tac) formation, the aim of which was to keep watch for hostile aircraft and for activity on the ground, while covering the blind spots behind other members of the formation. We flew about 100–200 yards out and 30° swept back from the leader at low level in a form of 'arrow' formation; later, when at the Tactical Weapons Unit (TWU), we had to learn how to lead this sort of formation ourselves. It was easy to maintain position in formation and keep the leader in view when on the outside of a turn, but it was more difficult on the inside. To maintain a safe

Hawk T.1A XX205 at the October 2005 Duxford Air Show. (Author)

BAe Hawk T.1A XX285/CB of 100 Squadron at RAF Coltishall on 17 September 2005. (Author)

height above the ground it was a fundamental rule never to fly below the leader. Additionally, speed had to be slightly reduced and the bank angle increased because of the smaller distance being travelled as compared with the leader. This resulted in those on the inside looking down the aircraft's nose at the leader, and it was then all too easy to lose sight of him under the nose. All this was supposed to be subordinated to the main aim of looking out for other aircraft, and as a result, the early tactical formation trips contained an element of danger for all concerned. In total I did six trips on tactical formation, and during May I achieved over thirty hours' flying, so the rate of training was fairly intensive.

The night-flying phase came in the middle of June, and consisted mainly of night circuits and landings plus night navigation exercises, using radio aids and visual navigation. In clear weather the latter was easy, as the lights of towns could be seen for miles. June was not the best time for night flying as we had to wait until about 11 p.m. for it to get dark, and even then the northern sky was still light. In all we did five flights – three dual and two solo. Then it was back to GH and IF consolidation trips in preparation for the final handling test in mid-July. I took mine with the chief instructor, and it consisted of a mix of low-level navigation, GH and simulated emergencies to increase the work-load. In spite of marginal weather, all went well and I passed this final test satisfactorily to earn my 'wings'. The course aerobatic competition came after the final handling test. Because of the high performance of the Hawk, it was not at low level and it took place over the Lleyn Peninsula, with a base height of 5,000 feet. Again I thought that I had a good chance, but the Hawk required a delicate touch to get the optimum performance by 'nibbling' on the edge of the pre-stall buffet during turns and pull-ups. Unfortunately, I pulled a little too far into the buffet, which made my aerobatics less crisp than they should have been. However, I reached the final fly-off and again achieved second place. This was another disappointment, but at least I had passed the course, coming second overall and had gained my wings. Coming second seemed to be my destiny, but I had to admit that Steve Hicks, the star of the course in most things, was an absolute ace.

During the course I had flown a total of eighty-two hours, including twenty-five solo. I was asked if I wished to become a Qualified Flying Instructor (QFI), which meant going straight to the Central Flying School for instructor training. This would have resulted in my returning to instruct at a flying training school as what was known as a 'creamed-off' instructor. While flattered at being asked, I had already decided that I wanted to join a front-line squadron, and therefore requested to go to RAF Brawdy in South Wales to fly on the RAF's last Hunter course at the Tactical Weapons Unit (TWU). My wish was granted, and along with several others I received a posting notice to report to Brawdy in September. Meanwhile I was presented with my wings by the Inspector of Flight Safety, Air Commodore Stonor, at the end of July. Shortly after I left Valley, a Hawk crashed while approaching to land. I had known the instructor and the student reasonably well. Apparently the aircraft rolled uncontrollably and they ejected very close to the ground at about 90° of bank. Sadly, the student was killed, but the instructor survived, albeit with major injuries to both ankles, as his parachute was only just opening when he hit the ground. He later recovered to go back to flying Jaguars.

As the course at Brawdy was not due to start until September, I was given a holding detachment to No. 1 Squadron at RAF Wittering, which was equipped with the Harrier GR3. This was my first opportunity to see a front-line fast jet squadron in action. The Falklands War had just ended, and the squadron, which had been involved in the operation, was just settling down after a spell of leave, so it was an interesting time. At the end of August I left for Brawdy, about ten miles north-west of Haverfordwest in South Wales, to join No. 1 TWU. No. 1 TWU trained pilots destined for the fast jet squadrons, and it consisted of two training squadrons, each of which carried the number of a former operational fighter squadron. No. 79 Squadron provided short (forty sorties totalling between thirty-three and fifty-three hours) refresher courses for experienced ground-attack pilots who were returning to flying following a ground tour, while 234 Squadron gave longer courses (sixteen weeks, and including thirty-six hours of solo flying) for pilots who had no previous ground-attack experience. A second TWU was based at Chivenor in Devon. I joined 234 Squadron with five other pilots, three of whom came straight from Valley and two from heavy aircraft – one from Nimrods and the other from Vulcans. The former Nimrod pilot eventually reached a Jaguar squadron, but the Vulcan pilot failed to make the grade on the Tornado GR1. As we were now in Strike Command, there was a change of pace as well as of emphasis in our training, and we had to learn to use the aircraft as a weapon rather than just flying it. The TWU was renowned for providing some of the best flying to be had, although Brawdy was also notorious for the bad weather that came off the Irish Sea. It was on high ground, very close to the coast, and the phenomenon of 40-knot fogs – really low stratus cloud – was not unusual.

Hawk T.1A XX309 at the May Air Show at Duxford in 2007. (Author)

We experienced our first disappointment on arrival: the Hunters were suffering from old age and associated serviceability problems, and were being withdrawn from service. Their task was taken over by the Hawk, albeit now painted green/grey instead of the red/white of training aircraft. As we were all experienced on the Hawk, there was a short ground-school phase, with just a quick refresher on the aircraft systems and an introduction to the weapons system. This comprised a single 30 mm Aden gun (later replaced by the ADEN 25 specified for the Harrier GR Mk 5) in a pod under the belly, with a practice bomb carrier ('carrier, bomb, light stores', or CBLS) under each wing, plus a gyro-stabilised gun/bombsight and associated weapons switches in the cockpit. Each CBLS could carry four 3 kg practice bombs, which produced a flash and smoke on impact with the ground, enabling the position of the bomb strike to be plotted on the weapons range. Although the gun pod alone did not produce much drag, the CBLS reduced low-level top speed from around 550 knots to just over 500 knots. Weapon safety was a very important aspect, which was drummed into us from the start. A master armament safety switch (MASS) was mounted on the cockpit coaming, and it was only set to 'live' when the aircraft was pointing down the runway for take-off. We speculated on what might

BAe Hawk T.1A XX285/CB of 100 Squadron on the line at RAF Coltishall on 17 September 2005. The squadron's motto, 'Sarang tebuan jangan dijolok', *is Malayan, and translates as 'Never stir up a hornet's nest'. All squadron Hawk aircraft are marked with the blue-and-gold chequers of the borough of Stamford either side of the fuselage roundel. These relate to a period in the 1950s and 60s when the squadron was based at Wittering. (Author)*

happen if the gun fired at this stage, since the nosewheel leg was directly in front of the gun; in reality we were pretty safe, as the weapons circuits were not finally made live until the undercarriage retracted.

I had my first trip in mid-September – this was a familiarisation flight to get back into practice after only two trips during the past couple of months. Next came an instrument flying check to ensure that we were safe to operate to our White Instrument Rating limits. Course flying then started with battle formation, which was normally flown at 420 knots. This was very different from tactical formation and was flown in pairs in line abreast approximately two miles apart, to enable each pilot to check the blind spot behind the other aircraft's tail. Because of the greatly increased distance between aircraft, it was initially very difficult to maintain the correct position in straight flight, since changes in speed and position relative to the leader were not immediately apparent. Turns were even more difficult, as, if both aircraft initiated a 90° turn simultaneously, one aircraft would end up either two miles ahead or two miles astern of the other, depending on the direction of turn. All turns were therefore called by the leader on the R/T, and the procedure for the 90° turn was for the pilot on the outside to start the turn, while the other pilot continued straight ahead for seven or eight seconds until he could see the other aircraft starting to slide behind his tail. He then started his turn, watching for the other aircraft to reappear from his 6 o'clock position and now on the inside of the turn, the inside pilot either tightening or slackening the final part of his turn so that when both aircraft straightened up after turning 90°, they were back in battle formation at two miles' separation.

For turns of less than 90°, as the outside aircraft started the turn, the inside pilot assisted by initially turning towards him until they were at about 90° to each other, before reversing the bank and flying the rest of the turn as for the 90° manoeuvre. (If the inside man did not 'assist the turn', he inevitably finished up ahead of his wingman.) If the turn was greater than 90°, the pilot on the inside continued straight ahead for less than the normal eight seconds before turning, while if a turnabout through 180° was required, both pilots simultaneously turned in the direction called by the leader at 2 'g' or more. To provide safe separation between aircraft, the pilot on the outside of the turn always pulled high to remove any possibility of collision, as the inside pilot inevitably lost sight of the other aircraft when it passed behind him. I discovered that it took a considerable amount of practice before I was reasonably competent at flying battle formation, and initially I frequently found that I trailed behind, or got ahead of the leader, or was too close or too far out. The first two flights were at medium level to allow the basic problems to be sorted out in safety, but later sorties were flown at low level. During the early flights, most of the time was spent watching other aircraft in the formation and trying to hold the correct position, to the detriment of the primary aim of searching the sky for hostile aircraft. However, with practice, battle formation became second nature and look-out was greatly improved. Even then, it still had its problems, especially if the weather deteriorated and the cloud was on the hill tops. The aircraft then had to revert to 'arrow' formation with wingmen about 100–200 yards behind and around 30° swept back on the leader so that they could follow him as he manoeuvred down twisting valleys. When back in clear weather the aircraft reverted to battle formation. As we only did four fifty-minute formation trips, two at medium level and two at low level, there was an awful lot to learn in a very short time.

Next came tracking exercises using the gyro gunsight. This sight was virtually the same as that used on the Meteor thirty years previously, and I initially found it just as difficult. The first three flights involved tracking another Hawk which was performing simple manoeuvres such as level turns and taking shots with the gunsight recorder camera by pressing the gun trigger. The Hawk had a powerful and sensitive tailplane control, and I found that tracking while adjusting the circle of ranging diamonds with the throttle twist-grip to enclose the target's wingtips required smooth and accurate flying and precise operation of the twist-grip. Rough handling caused the gunsight display (reticule) to bounce around on the sight screen as if it was on a piece of elastic.

A Qualified Weapons Instructor (QWI) debriefed the students after each sortie, using the film from the gunsight recorder camera, and gave a score for the percentage of time that the sight was tracking the target accurately. Having just about grasped the basics, we then went on to cine weave, in which the target aircraft performed a preset routine of turning, climbing, diving and rolling manoeuvres which the student following attempted to track. For this exercise the students flew in pairs – the first time that they were allowed to fly together without direct supervision – and they took turns as target and tracking aircraft. I found this exercise hard work, but achieved average results by the end of the phase, which covered four sorties. The tracking assessments were posted on the notice-board so that we could all see how everyone else was doing, and as far as the students were concerned this added to the pressure.

Hawk T.1A 345 at the May 2005 Duxford Air Show. (Author)

BAe Hawk T.1As XX285/CB and XX194/CL of 100 Squadron at RAF Coltishall on 17 September 2005. (Author)

A close-up view of the BAe Hawk T.1A cockpit. (Author)

After tracking came ground strafing with the ADEN 30 gun, and this I thoroughly enjoyed, as I classified it 'the sport of kings'. The Pembrey Range was on the Welsh coast, ten miles south of Carmarthen and less than ten minutes' flying time from Brawdy; the target was a fifteen-foot square canvas panel. The gun (which could fire 1,200–1,400 rounds a minute and had a muzzle velocity of 2,592 feet per second) was fired in a 10° dive, and the ideal firing range was 550–500 yards, with an absolute minimum of 450 yards, for a half-second burst of about ten to twelve rounds. Anything less than 450 yards resulted in a zero score and the possibility of being sent home by the Range Safety Officer (RSO). A microphone on the target recorded the 'crack' of shells passing within fifteen feet and gave an instantaneous readout of the score to the RSO, who relayed it to the pilot. The target range was judged by comparing the relative size of the aiming mark on the gunsight (an inverted 'T') with the size of the target. This was quite difficult as the range decreased very rapidly at 420 knots, with each half-second taking the aircraft 360 feet closer to the target. The minimum height on recovery was a hundred feet above the ground; this may not sound very low from a 10° dive, but for the first few times the ground seemed awfully close. The attack pattern used was quite fatiguing, to both aircraft and pilot. In those days a square pattern was flown at a height of 2,000 feet, pulling a 4 'g' turn at each corner. For the turn onto the firing run, 130° of bank was used to pull the nose down onto the target before rolling out on the firing heading; an oval pattern is now flown at lower 'g' levels to minimise fatigue counts on the life of the aircraft. Once steady in the dive, with the sight pointing close to the target, the pilot called 'in hot' or 'in dry' to the RSO to indicate whether he wanted to make a firing or a dummy pass. The RSO replied 'clear hot' or 'clear dry', as appropriate. Having confirmed 'clear hot', the pilot set the gun trigger safety catch to 'live', pulling the sighting mark onto the target as he approached. It was important to avoid starting to track too early, as this was likely to lead to over-controlling at the crucial time, and in a cross-wind it was necessary to aim into wind by a set number of feet per ten knots of wind component. With skill and experience, the pilot was later able to spot his rounds hitting the ground and determine the correction needed for the next pass. This required consistency to be able to put the sight exactly on the aiming point, and was not always possible at the student level of expertise. 'Spotting' the fall of their own rounds by students was frowned on, as it could delay recovery from the dive. On completion of the burst the pilot initiated a 6 'g' recovery into a 30°

Hawk T.1A XX184 at the Duxford September Air Show in 2008, painted in a green and brown camouflage scheme with '19' on the fin to represent the anniversary of the Spitfire, which made its service debut with 19 Squadron at RAF Duxford in 1938. (Author)

climb and made the gun trigger safe. Apart from pulling out at a safe height, the other major consideration was to avoid ricochets. Fired from a 10° dive onto wet sand, virtually all the shells ricocheted into the air beyond the target, and it was necessary to manoeuvre to avoid the 'ricochet hemisphere', which was the area where these shells were likely to be. Even so, there was still a small chance of collecting a shell, and about nine months later a Harrier GR3 crashed after a shell came through the windscreen, hitting the pilot. An exceptional pass produced ten hits or so, but anything greater than 50% was considered a good student score.

For the first sortie, the instructor pointed out the salient features of the Pembrey Range, and he then demonstrated a pattern, indicating the reference points on the ground. After this he made a couple of 'dry' (dummy) passes, before making a 'hot' (firing) pass. The student then had a go, initially with 'dry' passes until the instructor was satisfied that he was safe, and then 'hot'. The next two trips were solo, making 'dry' passes from which he had to bring back a good cine film to show competence and safety. Assuming that the QWI was satisfied at the subsequent cine debriefs, the student was cleared go 'hot' on the next solo sortie. I committed the most common of errors by firing out of range on my first solo sortie; this made it much more difficult to hit the target and get good scores, but at least it was safe. Apart from being physically demanding, range sorties had a high cockpit workload: a lot of things had to be done quickly, correctly and in the right order, and I found that it was starting to test the limits of my mental capacity. As many fast-jet pilots had previously discovered, quick reactions were not the prime requirement, but mental capacity. They need the ability to assess a mass of constantly changing information, prioritise it and act on it accurately and correctly without forgetting anything or becoming distracted. Individual capacity became the major factor assessed by staff throughout the course: by this stage we had all proved that we could fly reasonably well, and most pilots chopped (failed) at or after TWU were simply unable to cope with the high cockpit workload.

Dive-bombing, using a 10° dive and the same range pattern, followed on naturally from strafing. (On the Hawk's port wing inner pylon would be an ML Aviation CBLS 100 Mk 1 launcher for practice bombs. Typically, this is equipped with up to four Portsmouth Aviation 3 kg bombs which match the ballistic characteristics of retarded 1,000 lb bombs. On impact, they release brown smoke to enable the range officer to plot the position of bomb fall and so assess accuracy. Until it was withdrawn from RAF

Hawk T.1A XX307 'RAFBF – The Heart of the RAF', in red, white and black livery at the September Air Show at Duxford in 2007. (Author)

Hawk T.1A XX278/CD climbing high. (MoD)

combat use in the late 1980s, a MATRA 155 launch pod containing up to eighteen spin-stabilised rockets of 68 mm calibre was usually fitted beneath the Hawk's starboard wing.) The Hawk had a simple fixed sight for bombing, and during the pre-take-off brief, a 'sight depression' angle was calculated which took account of the forecast wind on the range and the particular bombing parameters to be used. In this case it was a 10° dive at 420 knots, with bomb release at 400 feet above the ground. Accurate flying and bomb release were essential, as if the bomb was released at a higher speed than planned it flew further than calculated, and vice versa. Sight depression was set to the calculated figure before engine start, then on arrival at the range the RSO gave the actual wind, and the sight was adjusted if necessary. As for strafing, the dual demonstration was followed by a 'dry' cine solo, though only one this time, and provided this was satisfactory the student was cleared for a 'hot' solo. The technique was to fly the same pattern as for strafing, and make similar R/T calls, but when cleared for a 'hot' run the 'pickle' button (bomb release) on the stick top was cleared for use by lifting its cover. The target was a circle of 75 ft radius, and as the aircraft approached, the range was assessed by comparing the relative size of the sight reticule to that of the target. The aim was to arrive at the correct height, speed, dive angle and range from the target before pressing the pickle button to release the bomb. If all four parameters were correct the bomb hit the ground well inside the circle; however, it was all too easy to get one or two badly wrong, and this resulted in a poor score. Direction was relatively simple, and left and right errors small: errors were mainly in distance, with the bomb falling long or short. A long bomb hit at 12 o'clock (beyond the target), while a short bomb hit at 6 o'clock (before the target).

The RSO scored each bomb and passed the result to the pilot – thus '70 feet at 6' (o'clock) meant seventy feet short of the target. Range to target was the most crucial factor, but the most common mistake was to fail to track the target steadily, letting the aircraft's natural stability cause the nose to gently pitch up as speed increased in the dive. Things went reasonably well on my first 'hot' sortie, and I achieved some passable scores, but on the next trip I dropped most of my bombs about 150 feet short, thus ruining my average. An experienced pilot would have recognised the error on his first bomb and corrected the later passes, but as an inexperienced student this was beyond me. The third and fourth solo trips combined dive-bombing and strafing; this was great fun, though hard work, and I passed the strafing and bombing phase satisfactorily.

A few of the other students had much better bombing scores than I did, and some were quite remarkable, with averages of only 20 ft miss distance. In mid-October, the course did two trips of night-flying in one night – one dual and one solo – just to keep in practice. From then on we did a mix of low-level navigation, level bombing and air combat. The initial low-level trip was to refresh on techniques, and we were then reintroduced to free navigation, which meant that the instructor nominated a new target during flight and the student had to navigate to it without any previous planning. Initially this was very difficult, as headings and distances had to be estimated simply by looking at the map, and times had then to be calculated by mental arithmetic. I had problems on the first couple of sorties, and was placed 'on review'. This was a formal action taken to allow the staff to give a student extra sorties above the normal syllabus, but it also put extra pressure on me, as it could be the start on the slippery slope to being failed. However, I was determined to succeed, and the next two trips went reasonably well, so to my great relief I was taken off review after about a week.

Meanwhile the course had moved on to level bombing at 200 feet and 420 knots. I soon found that it was more difficult to get good scores than in dive-bombing, despite the fact that speed and height were now constant instead of changing. Level bombing was very sensitive to any pitching movement at the moment of release, and it was easy to get bombs impacting short or long by 200 feet or more. The remedy was to fly very smoothly and ensure that the aircraft was in trim coming up to bomb release. An oval pattern was flown at 1,000 feet downwind, descending to 500 feet in the final turn, and then down to 200 feet on the run-in to the target. As the Hawk was not fitted with a radar

Hawk T.1A XX285 '1917–2007 90 Years', in yellow, blue and black livery at the September Air Show at Duxford in 2007. (Author)

altimeter, we used a very precise setting on the barometric altimeter. The RSO passed the local barometric pressure setting, accurate to the nearest tenth of a millibar, which should in theory provide a height which was correct to within a few feet. Smooth and accurate flying was then essential, as ten feet too high caused the bomb to impact fifty feet long, and vice versa. Initially, I found it very difficult, and my bombing scores were only average, although a couple of the others managed very good scores. Steve Hicks in particular produced some excellent scores. (I considered him to have been the only truly exceptional pilot that I had ever met.)

Air combat was the most enjoyable phase of the course. It was pure flying, and although it was physically hard work, the mental workload was not as high as in bombing or strafing, and it thus presented a welcome change. I particularly enjoyed air combat, and being a determined character did reasonably well at it. At that stage the Hawk was armed with only a gun, although it now has the capability to carry the AIM-9L Sidewinder air-to-air missile. The object was to get behind the opponent within gun range – less than 400 yards – and track

A Red Arrows' Hawk viewed from the cockpit. (RAF)

Apollo 1/4 Clover. (Author)

him to obtain film on the gunsight recorder camera. The training developed skills which we had already learned in tail-chases, aerobatics and tracking for cine weave. The early exercises involved only two aircraft, one versus the other (1-v-1), and the basic manoeuvres were first demonstrated by an instructor before the students had a go. The early combats were initiated from set-piece situations, such as starting from a position of advantage above and behind the opponent, or of disadvantage below and in front of him. Besides being more dangerous in a real situation, the latter was much more difficult, as apart from anything else it was harder to see the opponent when he was somewhere behind your tail and you were looking over your shoulder while pulling up to 6'g'.

The basic combat manoeuvres were given such exotic and descriptive names as the combat egg (any maximum-performance loop is egg shaped when viewed from the side) hi (high) and lo (low) yo-yos, and scissors. The combat egg described looping manoeuvres in which low speed and the earth's gravity increased the rate of pitch over the top, while the extra speed from the dive, plus the earth's gravity, reduced the maximum pitch rate at the bottom. The high yo-yo used the increased turning performance at the top of a high wing-over to advantage by cutting the corner on an opponent. The low yo-yo was the opposite: over-banking into a diving turn before pulling back up closed the distance to the opponent, but normally at the expense of an increased angle off. Each of these manoeuvres had a counter, and the pilot had to develop the skill of assessing what his opponent was doing, either to gain an advantage or at least to negate any advantage the opponent might have. This was quite difficult when he was some distance away. In 1-v-1 combat with well-matched aircraft it was necessary to try to make a small improvement in your situation with each manoeuvre and gradually build up an advantage. Trying to build too much advantage in one manoeuvre often resulted in losing out to the opponent. In a 'rolling scissors', both aircraft attempted to barrel-roll around each other, trying to lose ground and get behind their opponent. The scissors could be horizontal or vertical, in which case both aircraft ended up in a steep spiral dive. Flat scissors typically occurred towards the end of a combat, where both aircraft had run out of energy through weaving back and forth, each trying to get behind the other. Usually their speed was then low and they were near the ground, so that in real combat it was impossible to increase speed by diving. In training the base height – the minimum height allowed for safety reasons – was normally 5,000 feet. At this stage both aircraft would then be flying in deep buffet right on the edge of the stall, but it was still necessary to keep the nose up. Dropping the nose into a dive would either cause the aircraft to fly into the ground in a real dogfight, or break the safety base height in training. Even if this did not happen, any increase in speed caused one aircraft to get ahead of its opponent, giving the latter a decisive advantage. The last-ditch manoeuvre, or guns jink, was only undertaken when all other attempts to shake off an opponent from a gun-firing position had failed, and was basically a violent action to at least spoil his tracking and hopefully to throw him off the pursuit.

An important aspect of air combat was to be able to recognise early on when you were losing the battle. It might then be possible to break off completely, or pull away temporarily to rejoin the struggle with more energy, and preferably with an advantage. To be good at air combat required finesse, and the aircraft had to be flown smoothly, just nibbling into the pre-stall buffet to maintain maximum performance, without wasting energy in the form of speed or height. Height could be converted into speed and vice versa, but the important thing when in combat with an aircraft which had a similar basic performance was your energy level relative to that of your opponent.

When we had mastered the basics by starting with set-piece scenarios, the course moved on to free-play air combat. The exercise started with two aircraft flying parallel at about 12,000 feet and two miles apart; on the leader's call of 'outwards turn for combat – go', both aircraft turned away from each other by 45°. When we were five to six miles apart and the other aircraft appeared only as a small dot, the leader called 'inwards turn for combat – go', and each aircraft turned to head towards the other. For safety reasons, both pilots called 'tally' to confirm that they could see each other. If one pilot called 'no tally' they flew to pre-briefed safely separated heights. At this stage the fight was on and they were free to start manoeuvring to try to gain an advantage, although, as the aircraft came together, the pilots had to ensure that they achieved the minimum safe lateral separation of 1,000 feet.

A classic gambit was to pull up in a steep climb when passing the opponent in an effort to get above him, and then use the combat egg, pulling over the top of the loop at very low speed and hoping that he either fell out or went over the top at a lower altitude. In either case you were then well placed to get behind your opponent, but he would naturally be trying to do the same. From then on it was a case of assessing what he was doing and flying your aircraft to counter his moves and get behind him. In the Hawk, the pilots were normally pulling between 3 'g' and 6 'g', largely depending on the speed. Acceleration could drop to zero 'g' when 'unloading' the wing to zero lift and hence minimum drag, to gain energy before pitching back

into the fight. Negative 'g' was never used, as the simple counter was for an opponent to use his high rate of roll to get onto his back, where he would be pulling only a low amount of positive 'g' to track the aircraft pushing negative 'g'. Unlike the film *Top Gun*, where opposing aircraft always appear to be close together, range from the other aircraft was constantly varying from a minimum of about 1,000 feet to a maximum of several miles, where it appeared as just a dot. In these circumstances it was easy to lose sight of an opponent when he passed below, or against the deep blue of the sky above. This gave him a terrific advantage provided he could still see you, and the fight normally ended rapidly thereafter with his call of 'Fox 3, knock it off', which meant 'I am taking a gun's shot, stop the fight'. This reinforced the need to keep the opponent in sight as far as

Smoke On! The team has three display options, all of which are completely interchangeable and can change from one to another if the weather is variable. The Full Display takes place when the minimum cloud base is 4,500 feet; Rolling Display when minimum cloud base is 2,500 feet and Flat Display when minimum cloud base is 1,000 feet. (Author)

was possible and to predict where he was likely to reappear if he disappeared into a blind spot below or behind. It also emphasised the importance of building up a mental picture of where other aircraft were and the need to maintain situational awareness. During the early exercises it was all too easy to forget to check such important items as fuel state and the distance from base. These sorties pulling lots of 'g' were very tiring, but I really enjoyed this phase, particularly as I did reasonably well.

After six sorties of 1-v-1 air combat, I moved on to 2-v-1: that was two aircraft working together to kill one opponent. This was more realistic than 1-v-1, but it also emphasised the need for the pair to co-ordinate their actions if they were to get a quick kill. Normally, one of the pair engaged the opponent and kept him occupied, leaving the other pilot free to gain energy and get into an advantageous position. The preferred method of achieving the latter was for the free pilot to distance himself from the fight, keeping the duelling aircraft in view, but sufficiently far away for the opponent to lose track

Hawks of the Red Arrows climbing high. (RAF)

of him, rejoining the fight when an opportunity presented itself. Ideally he could then approach the single aircraft unsighted and, with a huge energy advantage, obtain a quick kill. The main problems were communicating clearly and concisely to your wingman regarding the rapidly changing situation, and getting far enough away from the fight before rejoining. Although 2-v-1 was excellent for teamwork and formation co-ordination and control, I always preferred 1-v-1 as the more basic form of the art, and for sheer fun.

Meanwhile, low-level navigation exercises were continued in conjunction with air combat trips. It was on one of these, when flying south through mid-Wales, that I came the closest I have ever been to having a mid-air collision. I crested a hill and met a Hunter doing the same thing, but going the other way. There was no time to do anything, and the Hunter passed about twenty feet above my canopy – so close that I heard the roar as it went past. This was rather a shock, and briefly scared me; fortunately I was later able to dismiss it as an expected hazard.

After the initial difficulties with navigation, I had regained my confidence following my good progress in air combat. The next phase covered simulated attack profiles (SAP), which were realistic missions with a pair of aircraft in battle formation attacking a target, using either the level or shallow-dive technique. After the first two SAPs, a simulated fighter was introduced to make a surprise attack or 'bounce' the pair. This was either another Hawk, or a Hunter from 79 Squadron, flown by a staff pilot who had details of their route and timings and intercepted them at various points along the route. These interceptions were made from various directions – high, low, head-on, astern, beam or quarter, – and the students endeavoured to see the bounce aircraft in time to evade him while continuing their progress to the target. If the chance presented itself, they were entitled to attack the bounce aircraft, although this was rare. The various directions of interception demanded different tactics to defeat the bounce aircraft. If he was seen at long range, the action was to turn away and run, calling 'buster' (go to full power) on the R/T, hoping that he had not seen them, and if he had, certainly before he got within missile range. Typically this was one-and-a-half miles if the bounce was astern, or up to three miles if he was on the beam. If the bounce was seen too late to be avoided, the pilot who saw him first made the R/T call 'counter port' or 'counter starboard', and the pair turned towards him at high 'g' and speed, aiming to pass him at the minimum safety separation of 1,000 feet. It was then extremely difficult for the bounce pilot to get a missile shot on either of the pair, as their exhausts were pointing away from the homing heads of his

(Left) 'I Do Love To Be Beside the Seaside': in this case at the annual Lowestoft Air Show. (Author)

heat-seeking missiles. Additionally, as he was being threatened, he now had to turn away to maintain minimum safe separation. After passing the bounce aircraft, the pair then maintained their course, running away from him, and as he now had to turn through 180° to take up the chase he had little prospect of catching them. This exercise demanded a good look-out and quick thinking to initiate the correct reaction and to make clear and concise radio calls. In these circumstances it was very easy to forget navigation and get lost, especially as the students were now navigating off the planned track. These missions produced a very high workload, especially if the weather, or just the visibility, was poor, making even large features difficult to see. The SAP built on techniques learned in low-level navigation, formation and 2-v-1 air combat, and it really became a test of mental capacity at times.

The Red Arrows climbing off Lowestoft beach during the annual two-day Air Show. (Author)

Towards the end of the SAP phase, we progressed to flying in formations of four aircraft, although initially these sorties were not bounced. These were flown in the old Hunter-style battle formation, with the element leaders, Nos 1 and 3, flying in line abreast and two miles apart, while their wingmen (Nos 2 and 4) flew about 30–40° swept back and 200 yards from their respective element leaders. The old dictum of 'stick to your leader, keep a good look-out and report any threats' was the basic brief for wingmen.

Finally, on our last trip before Christmas 1982, we graduated to a bounced four-aircraft formation, led by an instructor. This commenced with a hot first run attack (FRA) dive-bombing attack on the Pembrey Range, before routeing to make a simulated attack on an off-range target, while countering a bounce aircraft. The workload on this sortie was extremely high, but it was very exhilarating. Concurrently with the SAP phase, we started the final part of weapons training with what I considered to be the black art of air-to-air gun firing. The familiar pattern of dual demonstration and solo cine exercise was followed before we were allowed to fire the gun against a banner target. The banner, which was thirty feet long by six feet deep, was towed by a Hawk flown by an instructor on the end of 1,000 feet of cable at a speed of 200 knots over the Bristol Channel Range. There was really only one way to get consistently good scores, and that was to fly an accurate quarter attack to be at the correct range and angle off from the flag and to track steadily at the crucial time. Although it was an academic exercise as far as shooting down another aircraft was concerned, it did provide very useful training, as good judgement of speed and distance were required in setting up the attack pattern, while smooth and accurate tracking was essential if a reasonable score was to be obtained. From my initial efforts I was aware of the normal problems of either being too close to the flag at a high angle off and finding it impossible to track, or the alternative of doing a slack attack and ending up almost doing a stern attack on the flag. The instructor in the towing aircraft naturally kept a close eye on proceedings and was very quick to call 'stop, stop, stop' if a student appeared to be firing at too low an angle. This was potentially dangerous, as the shells would then be fired in the general direction of the towing aircraft, and if a student persisted with this type of attack he was sent home. The normal practice of dipping the tips of the shells in different-coloured paints was followed, to allow the score by each pilot to be counted after the flag was dropped back at Brawdy, and there was always close interest as the strikes were checked.

The Red Arrows taxiing at the Mildenhall Air Fête 2000. (Author)

On my first live firing sortie on 6 December, I scored no hits at all, but this was quite common for the initial attempt. My next air-to-air gunnery sortie was not until 4 January 1983, and I remember walking in after the trip, thinking I had obtained a satisfactory score, but nothing special. As I went to lunch, another student who was on the same detail claimed that he had peppered the flag, but when the flag was delivered to the squadron in the afternoon I discovered that I had scored twenty-two hits out of fifty rounds, which qualified as 'exceptional'. The other student had missed the flag completely. Having achieved average results for most of the previous weapons exercises and seen some of the other students get consistently better scores at strafing and bombing, it was gratifying to

The Red Arrows line up at the Mildenhall Air Fête 2000. (Author)

achieve good results. In the subsequent film debrief it was apparent that I had achieved accurate tracking at the correct range to obtain this result. The next sortie on the same day was not quite as good, but I finished overall in the 'exceptional' bracket, and this was an encouraging way to finish what for me had been a difficult course. In the four months I had flown sixty-six hours, which brought my grand total to just over 400 hours.

As with the previous training course, we then had to complete a form showing our three preferences for posting. At that time there was a choice of six different types of fast jet, each of which required a differing range of abilities. First came the single-seat types, with the Harrier as undisputedly the most demanding aircraft to operate. The Jaguar and Lightning came next, although many people considered that the Lightning was probably the more difficult, and the Lightning OCU certainly had a fearsome failure rate at times. The two-seat Buccaneer, Tornado GR1 and Phantom comprised the lower half of the list, as they all carried navigators, which reduced the pilot's workload. The Phantom force, however, had objected to always being at the bottom of the list, and as a result was now taking some very able pilots. Those considered not quite up to fast jets at this stage of their career, but who had shown potential, went to the small Canberra force. My choices all the way though training had been Harrier, Jaguar and Tornado. I preferred the low-level ground-attack role to air defence, and the Harrier was most pilots' dream aircraft. In the event, the final choice was governed by supply and demand. As I had done better at the air-defence skills, I changed my choices to Phantom, Jaguar and Tornado. In fact I would have been happy with any fast jet apart from the Buccaneer, since I did not fancy spending most of my time flying over the sea, which I thought might be rather boring. At the end of TWU there was a single 'role disposal board' for our course and for our compatriots from Valley on a parallel course at Chivenor. As it happened, I was selected for Jaguars. I was overjoyed at hearing the news, and in retrospect was pleased not to be going to the Phantom.

In January 1983 the MoD contracted for the modification of eighty-nine Hawks to expand the aircraft's weapons capability, and the resulting aircraft were designated T.Mk 1A. These could be armed with two AIM-9L Sidewinder AAMs on underwing launchers. For close-in air combat or ground strafing, a single 30 mm gun pod could also be fitted under the fuselage. The T.Mk 1A conversion programme was completed in May 1986, and the aircraft were intended as limited point-defence fighters for emergency use in the UK Defence Region to supplement the McDonnell Douglas Phantoms and Panavia Tornado F3s in the 'mixed fighter force'. A number of Hawk T.Mk 1 aircraft were rewinged, and a few of these aircraft were completed to T.Mk 1W and T.Mk 1 FTS standard to allow stores to be carried on two underwing hard-points, but not on the centre-line hard-point.

In 1977, meanwhile, BAe introduced the upgraded Hawk Mk 50 for an initial sale to Finland. That December four British-built aircraft were delivered, followed by forty-six assembled in Finland by Valmet. In December 1990 a follow-on order for seven Mk 51A aircraft was placed. In 1978 Kenya purchased twelve Hawk Mk 52s, and Indonesia acquired twenty Hawk Mk 53 aircraft. The Hawk Mk 60 that followed was powered by the more powerful Adour Mk 861 engine rated at 5,700 lb s.t. dry, additional wing leading-edge fences and four-position flaps to improve lift, anti-skid brakes and revised wheels and tyres. In July 1982 Zimbabwe ordered eight Hawk Mk 60 aircraft, and this was followed by another order for five Mk 60As. Dubai ordered nine Hawk Mk 61s and Abu Dhabi sixteen Hawk Mk 60s, of which fifteen were later upgraded to Hawk Mk 63A standard and supplemented by four Hawk Mk 63Cs. Kuwait ordered twelve Hawk Mk 64s, Saudi Arabia thirty Hawk Mk 65s, Switzerland twenty Hawk Mk 66s, including nineteen assembled by F+W, and South Korea twenty Hawk Mk 67 long-nosed aircraft fitted with ranging radar and nosewheel steering.

During the mid-1980s BAe could offer the Hawk Mk 100 based on the Hawk Mk 60 as a relatively cheap dedicated dual-role weapon-systems trainer and fully combat-capable ground-attack aircraft. This version was powered by the Adour Mk 871 turbofan rated at 5,845 lb s.t. dry, and its wingspan was increased by one foot nine inches to thirty-two feet seven inches, the extra length being at the tips to provide tip-mounted rails for two Sidewinder AAMs. The Hawk's wing was also adapted to take a larger warload by adding a degree of sweep-back (21.5° at the leading edge), so that the additional pylons accommodating the heavier ordnance loads required in the ground-attack role did not affect the Hawk's centre of gravity. The wing, which is stressed for six pylons carrying a maximum of 6,614 lb of stores, incorporates combat manoeuvre flaps. As well as wingtip AAMs, a single 30 mm ADEN cannon pod is an optional fitting on the fuselage centre-line in place of a

The Reds diving down to low off the sea at the Lowestoft Air Show. (Author)

The Red Arrows and the BAC Concorde take centre stage at the Mildenhall Air Fête 1984. (Author)

further stores place station. An elongated nose was added to house an optional forward-looking infra-red (FLIR) and/or laser sensors, and an advanced cockpit was equipped with multi-function displays and hands on throttle and stick (HOTAS), plus more sophisticated avionics to exploit its enhanced combat potential. The Hawk 100 first flew in October 1987 as a converted development airframe.

Abu Dhabi was the first customer for the Hawk Mk 100 series, with an order for eighteen Mk 102 aircraft with a radar warning receiver (RWR), wingtip launch rails and nose-mounted laser designator. In July 1990 Oman ordered four Hawk 103 aircraft, and that December Malaysia ordered ten Hawk 108s, of which the first was handed over in February 1994. The larger overseas order for the Hawk 100 came from Saudi Arabia, which, under the post-Gulf War 'Al Yamamah II' contract ordered up to sixty Hawk 100 aircraft. Indonesia ordered eight Hawk Mk 109s and Malaysia ordered ten Hawk 108s. In mid-1997 Australia ordered thirty-three Hawk 100-series aircraft to be delivered from 2000 as twelve British-built and twenty-one Australian-built aircraft, and in 1998 South Africa ordered twenty-four Hawk 100-series aircraft, both countries operating the aircraft as fighter lead-in trainers. Such was the international success of the Hawk two-seat models that BAe developed the Hawk Mk 200 single-seat variant to attract new customers, particularly the smaller air arms requiring a relatively cheap air-superiority fighter and ground-attack aircraft. The Hawk 200, which is also powered by the Adour Mk 871, is constructed of conventional aluminium alloy and has about 80% commonalty with the two-seat models. Compared to the short-term option of continual refurbishment of older aircraft, it is a far more cost-effective package in the long term, not least because it does not require trained navigators to occupy second seats. While redesigning the Hawk's forward fuselage to accommodate a single cockpit, BAe also made provision for a Northrop Grumman (originally Westinghouse) APG-66H radar, a multi-mode equipment modified from that fitted in the Lockheed Martin F-16, and an inbuilt pair of 25 mm ADEN cannon under the cockpit floor. With the pilot's seat set further aft than the forward position of other Hawks, the pilot faces a main instrument panel that includes a comms/navigation integration panel, HUD, multi-function CRT display, radar display configured for the most modern symbology, and a radar homing and warning system to display enemy radar signals (RHAW) receiver. Provision was made also for seven hard-points (including wingtip AAM launchers) which enables 6,614 lb of stores, the same as the load of the Hawk 100, to be carried.

The Hawk 200 demonstrator (ZG200) flew for the first time on 19 May 1986, and was lost a month later in a flying accident, almost certainly resulting from momentary loss of pilot orientation under high 'g' loads. The second Hawk 200, which flew on 24 April 1987, differed in having full avionics but no radar. Eventually, this aircraft received the fuselage-mounted tailplane vanes, or side-mounted under root fins (SMURFs) developed for the US Navy's T-45 Goshawk trainer, which are designed to counteract any tendency for the tailplane to stall. These vanes throw a vortex over the tailplane to prevent undue travel caused by downwash from the flaps when the aircraft is in the low-speed configuration. In addition, an RWR was fitted to the fin leading edge, and the rear fuselage brake chute 'box' was deepened to accommodate a chaff/flare dispenser and rearward-facing RWR antenna. The first APG-66-equipped Hawk 200 RDA (Radar Development Aircraft) first flew on 13 February 1992. Two years earlier, on 31

July 1990, Oman became the launch customer for the Hawk 200 when it ordered twelve Mk 203 aircraft, mainly as replacements for its ageing Hawker Hunters. On 10 December 1990 Malaysia was next with an order for eighteen Hawk 208s. In June 1993 Indonesia ordered the first of thirty-two Hawk 109 two-seaters and Hawk 209 single-seaters, but not all of these were delivered because of Indonesia's financial problems and international pressure concerning its 'human rights' record.

Meanwhile, in November 1981 the US Navy concluded an evaluation of available training types for the US Navy experimental training system (VTXTS) programme by selecting a modified version of the Hawk trainer, which was superior in many respects to that of competing aircraft, as the aircraft component of its T45 training system. This was aimed at the production of up to 600 jet pilots annually throughout the 1990s and into the twenty-first century. In May 1986 an engineering development contract was awarded to McDonnell Douglas as the US prime contractor. The principal subcontractor is BAe, which retains responsibility for the wing, centre and rear fuselage, fin, tailplane, windscreen, canopy and flying controls. Initially, the requirement was for two versions, the T-45A for carrier-borne operation and the T-45B for land-based training and dummy carrier landing practice, but extending the airframe hours of both the Rockwell T-2B/C Buckeye intermediate trainer and McDonnell Douglas TA-4J Skyhawk advanced trainer led to a USN decision to acquire only the T-45A with full carrier qualification. The T-45A, which was renamed Goshawk to avoid confusion with the US Army Hawk surface-to-air missile, is a land-based aircraft, flying to a training carrier as required. The original total of 268 aircraft was later reduced to 197 production Goshawks.

Black Hawks

Based at RAF Leeming in North Yorkshire and equipped with Hawk fast-jet training aircraft, 100 Squadron, colloquially known as 'The Ton', is home to the RAF's Navigator Training Unit, which produces weapon systems officers (WSOs) for the front-line Tornado and Eurofighter squadrons. In addition, A and B Flights provide support flying for the rest of the RAF. The primary role is particularly varied: the support of all front-line RAF flying units and radar sites, and participation in major training exercises as 'aggressor'

The Red Arrows and the BAC Concorde – an unbeatable combination! (Author)

forces. The squadron is also frequently tasked to support the continued development of the airborne radar in the Eurofighter Typhoon, and it also has a number of secondary roles – the advanced training of RAF fast-jet weapons systems operators destined for the Tornado F3 and GR4, and the training of UK and foreign forward air controllers. The black Hawks can simulate a wide variety of aircraft and tactics required for specific training purposes, and they regularly provide agile, visual fighters for air-combat training, thus making a vital

The Synchro Pair's famous inverted pass. (Author)

contribution to the operational training programmes of all front-line squadrons. In a typical day, the wide variety of tasking could include sending a pair of Hawks to engage in air-combat training with Jaguar aircraft, providing a 'bounce' aircraft to act as an enemy to attack a formation of Tornado GR4s on a low-level bombing sortie, or completing affiliation training with multi-engine or rotary-wing aircraft to enable their crews to gain experience of operating against fast-jet aggressors. Further to this, the squadron assists in the training of fighter controllers by generating 'friendly' and 'enemy' aircraft to allow trainee fighter controllers to direct real-time intercepts and visual identification procedures.

'The Reds'

Last but not least, the most famous operator of the Hawk is of course the Red Arrows, part of the Central

Flying School at RAF Scampton, whose primary role in peace is to demonstrate the teamwork and excellence of performance demanded of all RAF personnel. The nine pilots have varying backgrounds and are a cross-section of the Royal Air Force's fast-jet aircrew. Between them they have amassed 24,000 flying hours, and most have served for at least ten years in the Royal Air Force. The tour on the Red Arrows is normally three years, after which the pilots return to front-line or instructional duties. The changing of three pilots each year is the best compromise between the injection of 'new blood' and maintaining a stable, experienced foundation, on which to build the next year's display. Early October is the time when the three new pilots who have joined the team

Five in formation with the Synchro Pair detached. (Author)

Pulling up! (Author)

commence their work-up. They will have flown in the rear seat behind an experienced team pilot for the last month of the display season, gleaning valuable tips about formation display flying and the various techniques involved. The initial weeks are spent converting to the Hawk and looping and rolling in small formations above the airfield. As proficiency grows, so the height is lowered and the formations increase in size. The first proper day of practice can prove both exhilarating and exhausting. After an extensive brief on formation positions, visual references and radio calls, the pilots are ready for their first formation ride. It all starts gently enough, but soon the four-aircraft formation has achieved its first loop and roll. Safely back on *terra firma,* their flying-suits are damp from the physical exertion and necks are slightly stiff from staring over shoulders. 'At times, you thought you would crush the control column into white powder', the new pilots say.

Trying to relax proves difficult as these early sorties are all run on pure adrenalin. From now on it is practice, practice, practice: three times a day; five days a week. The pace seems relentless. Slowly, your experience and confidence grows, as does the repertoire of basic formation aerobatic manoeuvres. Soon, the Boss brings his gaggle of new boys over the airfield to run through a simple acrobatic sequence. Many critical eyes follow your progress and everything from here on is recorded on video tape. The real debriefing can now begin, for the video proves invaluable. What may feel right in the air does not always look right from the ground, and it is on the ground where many thousands of people will soon be judging you. Some days you wonder if you will ever be able to manage it; the most basic manoeuvres can sometimes seem impossible. Only by constant practice and self-criticism will you progress. So how does all this compare with the front-line flying you have left behind? The Hawk trainer proves rugged, reliable and much simpler to fly and operate than your last mount. This allows you to use all your concentration on the job in hand, rather than worrying about the complexities of weaponry and advanced avionics. Your more experienced compatriots in their second and third years with the team agree. The Hawk has proved to be more than ideal for the role of formation aerobatic flying. The controls are light and responsive and the aircraft is a stable mount – the ideal combination of characteristics for formation work. As with many turbofan engines, the Hawk's Adour powerplant can have a rather slow response to throttle

Join-Up Loop to Parasol Break (Finale) (Author)

movements. This poses few problems to other training units, but to overcome the limitation to aerobatic flying, the Red Arrows' aircraft have a modified fuel system to give the engine a much-improved engine response time. Thrust is good, and during the majority of the display, engines are throttled back to prevent the speed from building up excessively. Flying controls are power assisted, requiring little physical effort from the pilot, and the Hawk possesses forgiving flying characteristics. Aircraft are stressed to +8 and -3–5 'g', and with the very low drag exerted by the wing, the turning performance is similar to that of the vaunted F-16 Fighting Falcon. During aerobatic flying, however, a practical limit of 5 'g' is imposed. The Synchro Pair are the two team members who pull the most during the display – flying to the aircraft's limits at only a hundred feet above the ground with complete confidence in their aeroplanes. Responsive controls allow quick and accurate corrections to be made, so allowing the Red Arrows to achieve the polished performance which is their hallmark.

By mid-November the work-up has progressed to formations of seven aircraft, allowing servicing to be carried out on some of the aeroplanes, without any loss of value to the pilot work-up. By the New Year, all of the aircraft are available and the pilots are ready to fly nine-aircraft formations. Meanwhile, deep servicing of the aircraft is carried out in rotation so that the pilots' training sorties can progress uninterrupted up to three times a day, five days a week. By early February, all of the aircraft are available and the pilots are ready to fly nine-aircraft formations. The team can now concentrate on developing a display sequence. Several new ideas will have been tried during the winter; some more successful than others! The winter work-up culminates with a detachment to Akrotiri, in Cyprus, where fine weather guarantees continuity of flying and allows the final polish to be put on the display. The display sequence is then performed in front of the Commander-in-Chief Royal Air Force Support Command, who must give his approval before the team can display before the public.

Back in the UK the time has now come to get the show on the road for the summer's season, and six months of hectic activity begin early in April. The full display sequence, flown in good weather, demonstrates twenty-three different formation manoeuvres. The pilots recall:

Such is the concentration required to hold precise formation references during manoeuvres – smoke

'Seaside Special' at the annual Cromer Air Show on the Norfolk Coast. (Author)

'End of the Pier Show', with spectacular formation aerobatics to thrill the holiday crowd at the annual Cromer Air Show. (Author)

on; smoke off; change smoke colours; move quickly in, out, forward or backward; listen to R/T calls; make your own calls. There simply isn't time to gaze out of the canopy and view the scene below. On a normal display, especially for positions like Red 4, 5, 8 or 9, there are three or four times when the crowd falls naturally into your field of view for a couple of seconds. Then you can see if you are displaying before a thousand or two, or tens of thousands, but the crowd is just a sea of colours and becomes part of the scenery. Surprisingly, what sometimes you can see are the bursts of light from hundreds of camera flash guns on an overcast day. If you are flying from the same airfield as the display, there may be a long taxi out to the holding point of the runway, and you can pass along the crowd line as you prepare for take-off. It is only then that you realise just how many people will be watching the display – and possibly your mistakes! By far the hardest crowd of all to fly for is a large gathering of your fellow pilots, who know what is going on and can 'see' into your cockpit. Never expect sympathy from other such hard-nosed professionals.

As the season goes on, the initial flush of excitement at performing in front of a big crowd passes, and size becomes a secondary consideration. On the bottom line, the display itself takes the form of a relentless search for perfection within the team. Ultimately, members become their own severest critics, finding that the immediate audience for each of their sorties is just eight other pilots. So, as the first of your three seasons with the Red Arrows draws to a close, you find yourself completely settled in the team, and confident of your ability to pull your weight. Soon there will be another hopeful pilot sitting behind you, experiencing the same apprehension as you once did, now seemingly aeons ago. The job is demanding, but immensely satisfying, and at times like this you realise how fortunate you are to be enjoying your work so much. All in all, as in its other roles, the Hawk will be a difficult act to follow when the time comes for its replacement.

In December 2004, a £158 million contract was placed for the next-generation Hawk aircraft, the Hawk 128 AJT (Advanced Jet Trainer). The Hawk 128 introduces student pilots to the digital cockpit environment that they will experience in front-line operational service, and provides a seamless transition between basic flying training and operational conversion training onto advanced fighter aircraft such as the Typhoon F2 and the Joint Combat Aircraft.

PROFILES OF FLIGHT

BRITISH AEROSPACE HAWK

HAWK T1, T1A, T1W, 102D, 115(C T-115), 120LIFT, 120D, 127LIF, 200RDA

Hawk T.Mk 1 XX238 '238' of the **Central Flying School**
1986 display aircraft

Hawk T.Mk 1 XX162 '162' of No.4 Flying Training School
1980

Hawk T.Mk 1 XX172 of the St Athan Station Flight
Special scheme 1995

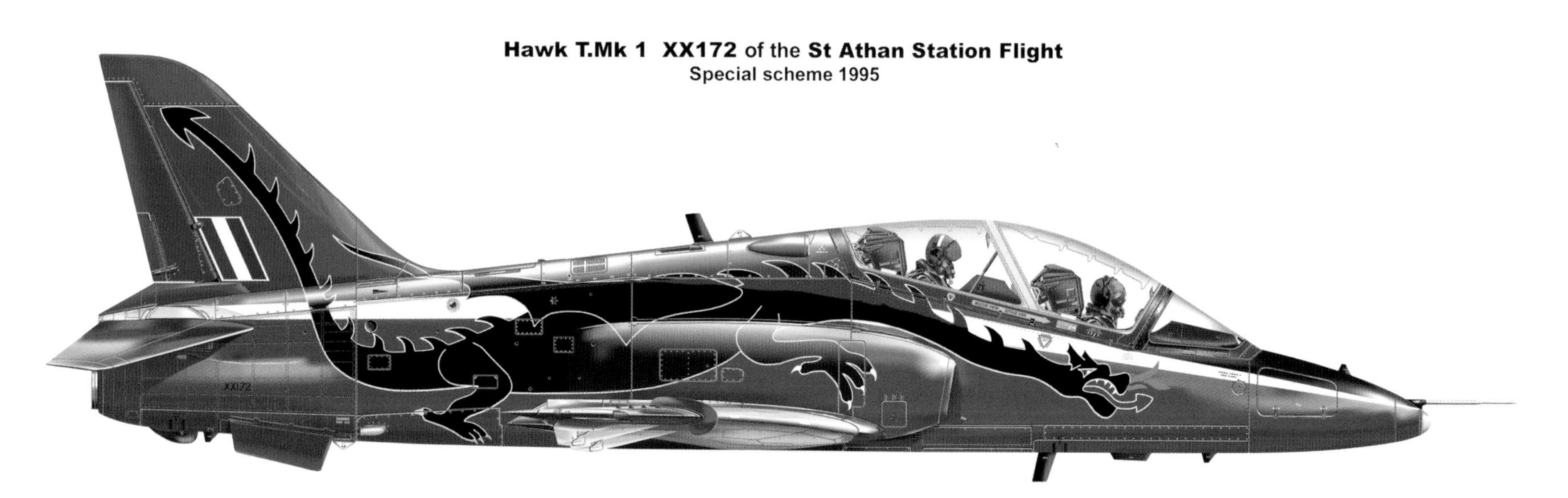

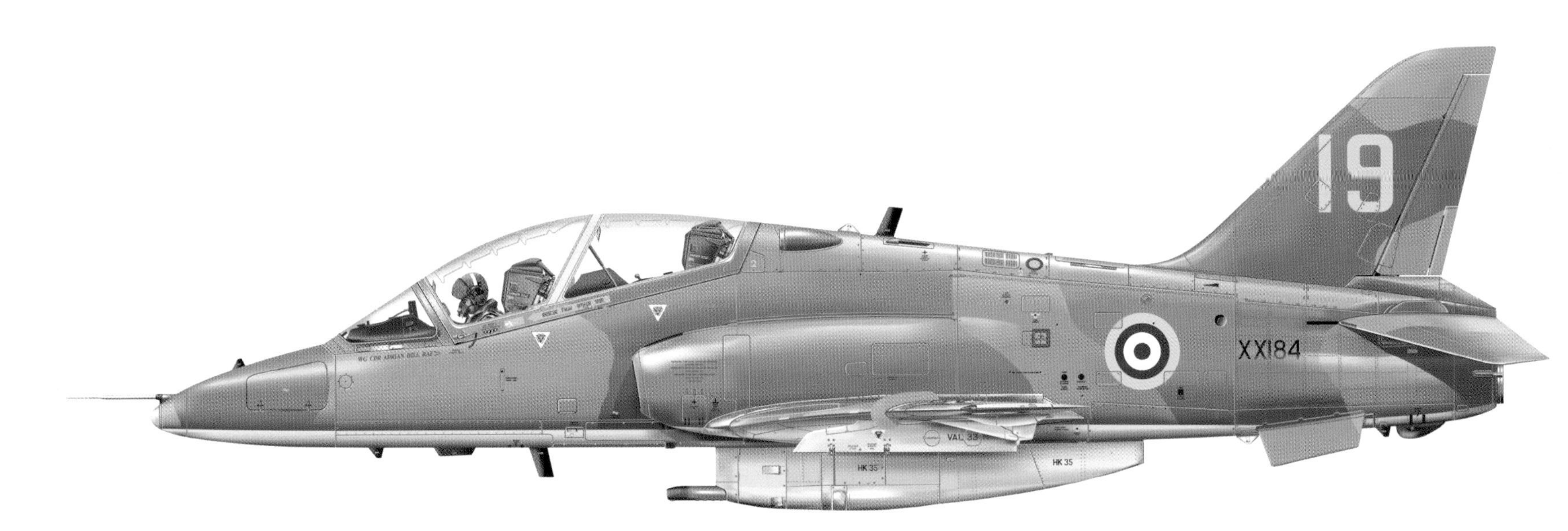

Hawk T.Mk 1A XX184 '19' of **No.19 (Reserve) Squadron**
70th anniversary of the Spitfire entering service 1938 - 2008

Hawk T.Mk 1W XX195 of No.4 Flying Training School
85th anniversary 1921 - 2006

Hawk T.Mk 1A XX205 of **No.208 (Reserve) Squadron**
90th anniversary 1916 - 2006

Hawk T.Mk 1A XX261 of **No.4 Flying Training School**
30th anniversary of the Hawk 1974 - 2004

Hawk T.Mk 1A XX285 of No.100 Squadron
90th anniversary 1917 - 2007

Hawk T.Mk 1 XX295 '295' of **No.4 Flying Training School**
1992

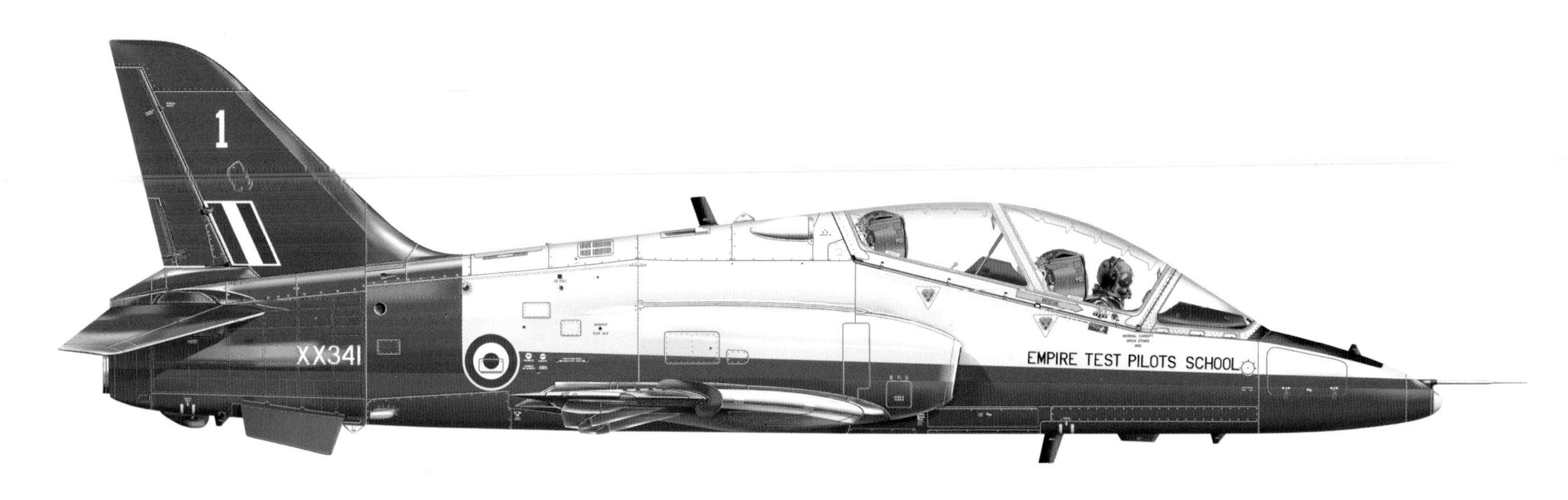

Hawk T.Mk 1 XX341 '1' of the **Empire Test Pilots School**
1983

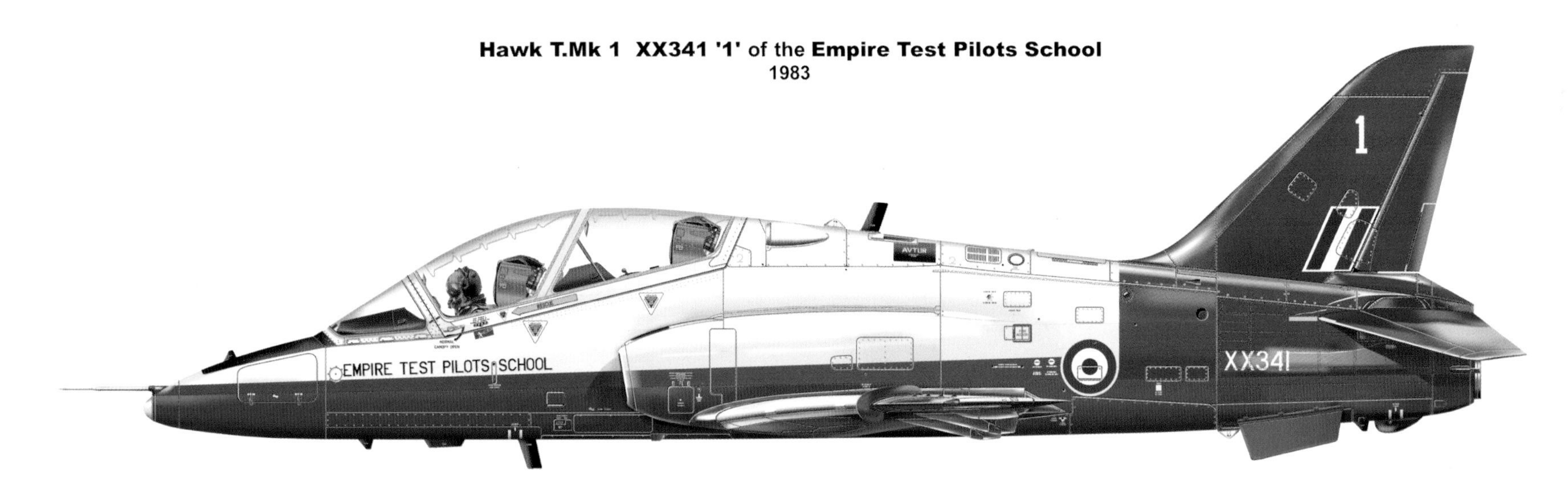

Hawk T.Mk 1 XX341 '1' of the **Empire Test Pilots School**
Advanced Stability Training & Research Aircraft 2005

Hawk Mk 102D ZJ100
Production prototype and demonstrator 2000

Hawk Mk 120D ZJ951
Demonstrator 2008

Hawk CT-155 155221 of **NATO Flying Training in Canada**
(Hawk Mk 115)
NFTC Phase IV tactical fighter pilot training

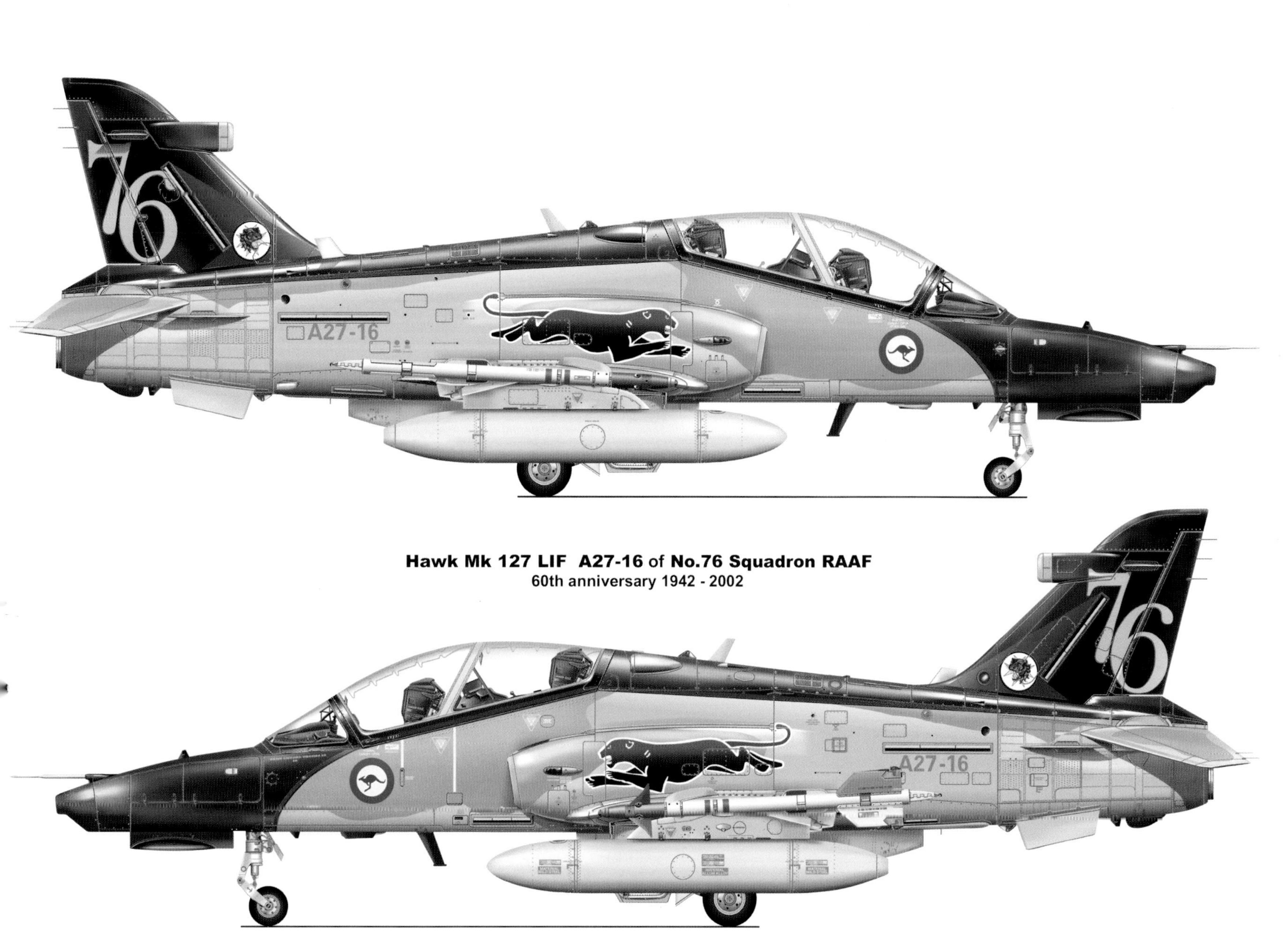

Hawk Mk 127 LIF A27-16 of **No.76 Squadron RAAF**
60th anniversary 1942 - 2002

Hawk Mk 127 LIF A27-21 of **No.79 Squadron RAAF**
60th anniversary 1943 - 2003

Hawk Mk 120 LIFT 271 of No.85 Combat Flying School SAAF
Display aircraft 2008

Hawk Mk 200RDA ZJ201 '294'
Demonstrator 1999